SIMPLY **SCIENCE**

The Simple Science of

LIGHT

by Emily James

CAPSTONE PRESS

a capstone imprint

A+ Books are published by Capstone Press,
1710 Roe Crest Drive, North Mankato, Minnesota 56003
www.mycapstone.com

Library of Congress Cataloging-in-Publication Data
Cataloging-in-publication information is on file with the Library of Congress.
ISBN 978-1-5157-7082-4 (library binding)
ISBN 978-1-5157-7089-3 (paperback)
ISBN 978-1-5157-7096-1 (eBook PDF)

Editorial Credits
Jaclyn Jaycox, editor; Jenny Bergstrom, designer; Jo Miller, media researcher; Tori Abraham, production specialist

Photo Credits
Shutterstock: DVarela, back cover, Gelpi, 10-11, Horiyan, 29 (inset), Len Green, 20-21, Monkey Business Images, 27 (inset),
moomsabuy, 11 (inset), nednapa, 22-23, Okhotnikova Ekaterina, 4-5, Perry Correll, 17, PointImages, 16, PongMoji, 28,
rck_953, 18-19, Ronnachai Palas, 14-15, Ruslan Guzov, 7, Suzanna Tucker, 24-25, Suzanne Tucker, 8-9, Trong Nguyen,
26-27, WileeCole Phototgraphy, 29 (left), XiXinXing, 25 (inset), Yuganov Konstantin, 6, Zurijeta, 12-13

Design Elements
Shutterstock: Macrovector, Skylines

Note to Parents, Teachers, and Librarians

This Simply Science book uses full color photographs and a nonfiction format to introduce the concept of light. *The Simple
Science of Light* is designed to be read aloud to a pre-reader or to be read independently by an early reader. Photographs
help listeners and early readers understand the text and concepts discussed. The book encourages further learning by
including the following sections: Table of Contents, Glossary, Read More, Internet Sites, and Index. Early readers may
need assistance using these features.

Printed in the United States of America.
010374F17

Table of CONTENTS

Delightful Light

Your shadow plays on a sunny day.
Water sparkles and shines. At a storm's
end, a rainbow bends.

Wherever you look, light dazzles and
dances. It makes wonderful shapes
and colors.

Light lets you see things. The brighter the light, the more you can see. Without light, you cannot see anything.

You see an object when light bounces off it. Do you sometimes see shadows and shapes in a dark room? If so, a bit of light is sneaking in!

Where Does Light Come From?

Light comes from the sun. It is so bright that we can even see on cloudy days. Lightning, fireflies, and the northern lights also make natural light.

At night we may make our own light
to see. We may turn on light bulbs.
We may make a fire.

What Makes Shadows?

Light travels in rays. See the streams of light shooting out of a movie projector in a dark theater? See the beam shining from a flashlight?

A spot of darkness forms when a
solid object blocks light rays. This spot
is called a shadow. Shadows fall behind the
object blocking the light.

Your body is a solid object. On a sunny day, it blocks the sunlight's path and forms a shadow. The sun can shine *on* you, but it can't shine *through* you.

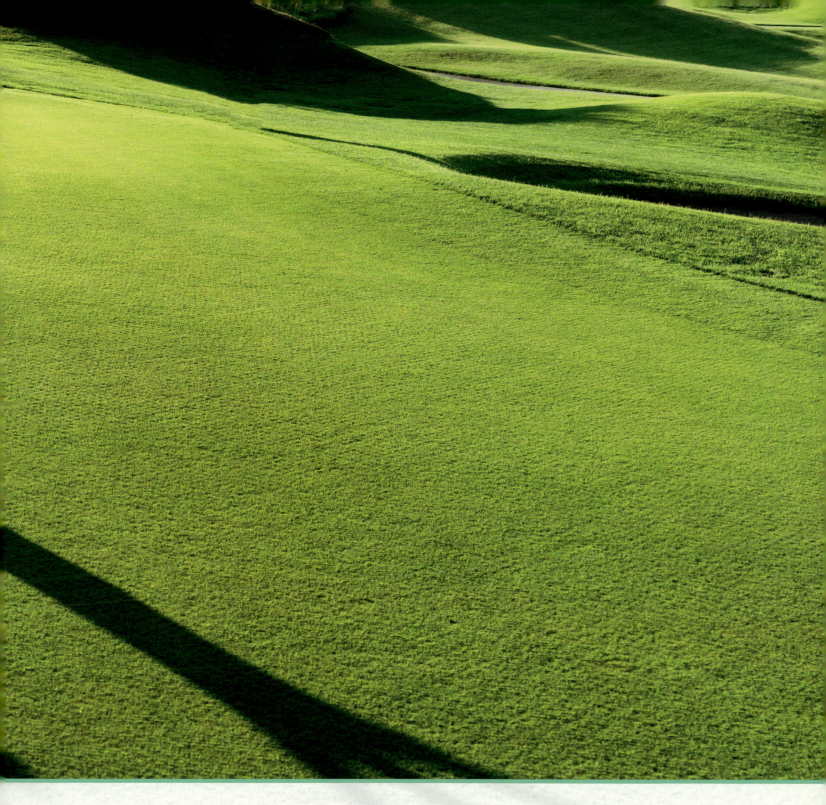

Walk toward the sun, and your shadow is behind you. Walk away from the sun, and your shadow is in front of you.

All About Reflections

Everything you see reflects light, including trees, cars, and people. Without reflected light, we can't see. Some objects reflect more light than others.

When light hits something smooth and shiny, most of the light rays bounce off it. Look in a mirror. Light rays are bouncing from you to the mirror and back again. Your image is a reflection.

Reflections aren't seen only in mirrors.
They appear all around your house!

Look at a shiny spoon or a silver toaster.
Can you see yourself? Look at a black TV
screen. Do these reflections look different
from the one in the mirror?

The moon has no light of its own. It's lit
by the sun. Moonlight is light reflecting off
the moon.

At night, the reflection lights your path.
It paints the trees silver. It makes
buildings glow.

How Are Rainbows Made?

A ray of sunlight is like a rope that's made of many strands. Each strand has its own color: red, orange, yellow, green, blue, or violet.

After a storm, water droplets fill the air.
When sunlight shines through them,
the rays bend. As they bend, all the colors
in the rays separate. A rainbow forms!

You might even see a rainbow on a cloudless day. Look closely at a soap bubble. See the rainbow?

Find a rainbow in the spray of a garden hose. You can also see rainbow colors in a sparkling diamond.

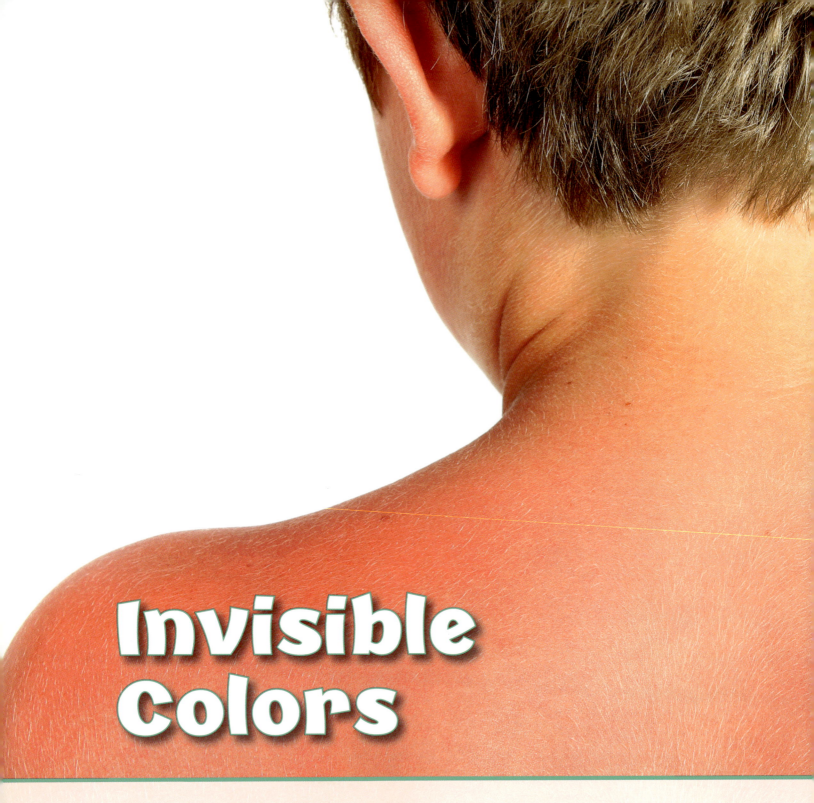

Invisible Colors

There are some colors of the rainbow that people can't see. They are called infrared light and ultraviolet light. We feel infrared light as heat. Anything that gives off heat has infrared light.

24

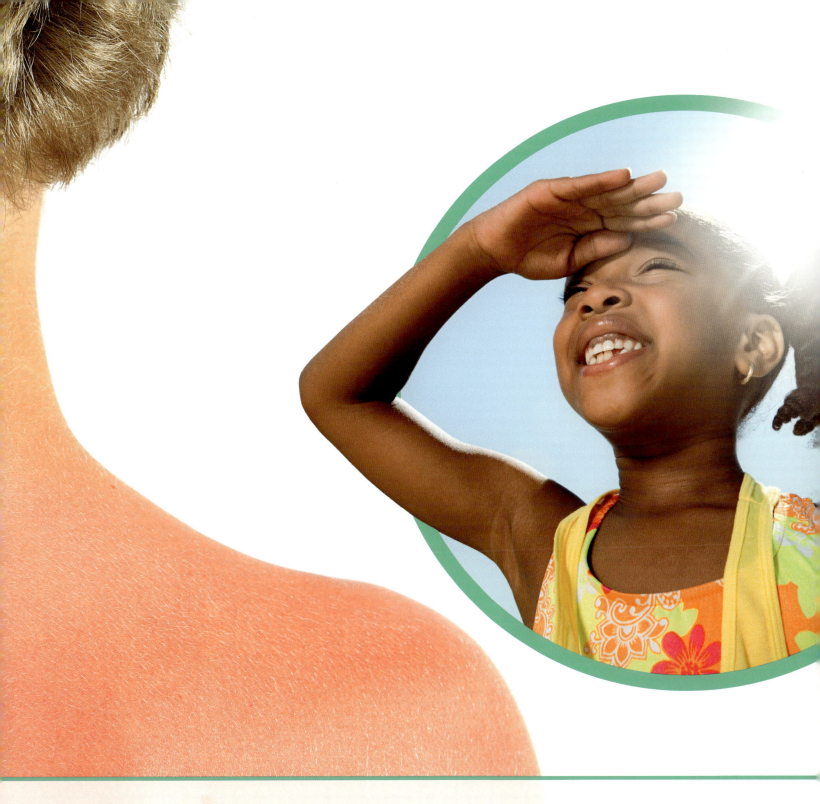

The sun, a warm sidewalk, and even your body all have infrared light. The sun also gives off a lot of ultraviolet light. This is the light that makes sunburns. Ouch!

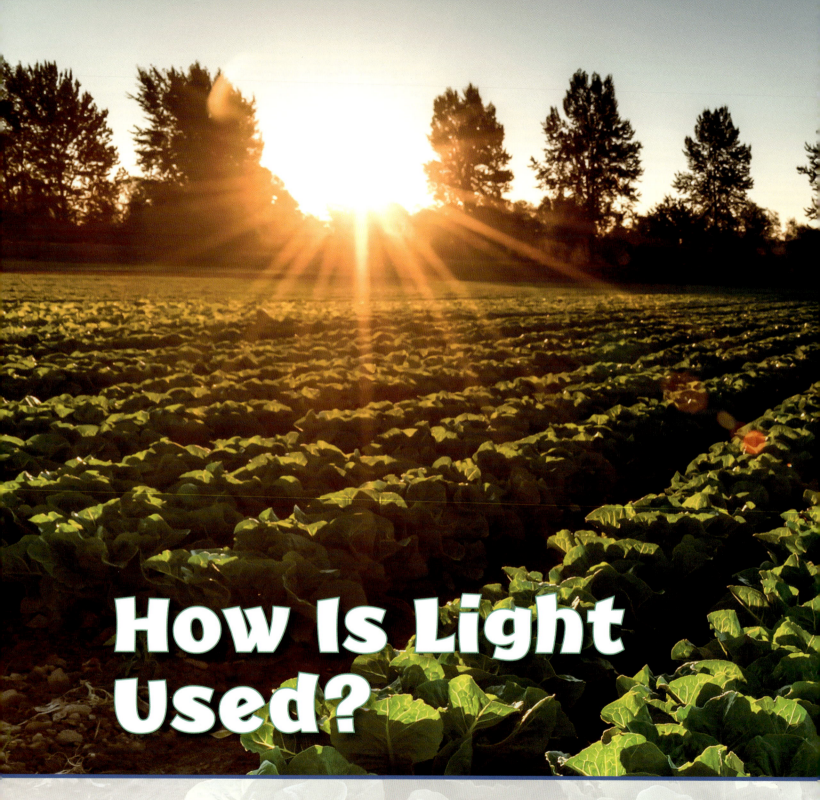

How Is Light Used?

Light is a big part of our lives. We need it to work and play. Without light, plants couldn't grow. Without plants, we wouldn't have any food to eat.

All around us, light is
sparkling, swirling, and blinking. It's
bending and bouncing. Watch! Wonder!
See all the colorful things to explore!

Make a Rainbow!

Rainbows are amazing! They are full of color and seem to appear out of nowhere. Try this fun activity to see if you can make your very own rainbow!

What You Need:

a bowl a small mirror
water white paper

What You Do:

- Fill a bowl with water and put it in a sunny spot.
- Place a mirror in the bowl, with its shiny side facing the sunlight. Be careful not to look at the sun in the mirror!
- Lean the mirror against one side of the bowl so it is standing up. (If it won't stand by itself, hold it with your hands.)
- Have a friend hold a piece of white paper outside the bowl, across from the mirror.
- What do you see on the white paper? How did it get there? Try tilting the mirror a bit. What happens?

GLOSSARY

beam—a ray or band of light from a flashlight, a car headlight, or the sun

infrared light—light that produces heat; humans cannot see infrared light

northern lights—bright, colorful streaks of light that appear in the night sky in the far north

projector—a machine that shows movies on a screen

reflect—to return light from an object

separate—to set, put, or keep apart

shadow—the dark shape made when something blocks light

strand—a small, thin piece of something that looks like a string

ultraviolet light—an invisible form of light that can cause sunburns

READ MORE

Dunne, Abbie. *Light*. Physical Science. North Mankato, Minn.: Capstone Press, 2017.

Johnson, Robin. *What Are Shadows and Reflections?* Light and Sound Waves Close-Up. New York: Crabtree Publishing Company, 2014.

Pfeffer, Wendy. *Light Is All Around Us.* Let's Read and Find Out Science. New York: HarperCollins Publishers, 2014.

INTERNET SITES

FactHound offers a safe, fun way to find Internet sites related to this book.

All of the sites on FactHound have been researched by our staff.

Here's all you do:

Visit *www.facthound.com*

Type in this code: 9781515770824

 Check out projects, games and lots more at **www.capstonekids.com**

CRITICAL THINKING QUESTIONS

1. At night, we need to make our own light to see. Name three ways you can make light.
2. The moon has no light of its own. How does it light up at night?
3. The sun gives off ultraviolet light. What is it? Hint: Use your glossary for help!

INDEX